GANDHI

Lifelines

For Josué

GANDHI

Lifelines

TEXT BY MOHANDAS K. GANDHI

EDITED AND ILLUSTRATED
BY BEATRICE TANAKA

Text copyright © Navajivan Trust. By the permission of the Navajivan Trust,
Ahmedabad—380 014 (India)

Compilation and illustration copyright © 1997 Beatrice Tanaka

Published in the United States by
Four Walls Eight Windows
39 West 14th Street
New York, NY 10011

U.K. offices:
Four Walls Eight Windows/Turnaround Distribution
Unit 3 Olympia Trading Estate
Coburg Road, Wood Green
London N22 6TZ

All rights reserved. No part of this book may be reproduced, stored in a database or other retrieval system, or transmitted in any form, by any means, including mechanical, electronic, photocopying, recording, or otherwise, without the prior written permission of the publisher.

Library of Congress Cataloging-in-Publication Data:
Gandhi
p. cm
ISBN 1-56858-088-6 (pbk.)
1. Gandhi, Mahatma, 1869-1948--Quotations. 2. Gandhi, Mahatma, 1869-1948--
Pictorial works.
DS481.g23G29 1997

954.03'5'092--dc121   96-48609
                                                              CIP

10 9 8 7 6 5 4 3 2 1
Printed in the United States
Book design by Big Fish

Gandhi was inevitable.

If humanity is to progress, Gandhi is inescapable.

He lived, thought, and acted, inspired by the vision

of humanity evolving toward a world

of peace and harmony.

We may ignore him at our own risk.

Dr. Martin Luther King, Jr.

The real question is to bring about man's highest intellectual, economic, political, and moral development.

I would develop in the child his hands, his brain, and his soul.

The hands have almost atrophied.

The soul has been altogether ignored.

Gandhi's Light

We really live through and in our work.
We perish through our perishable bodies
if instead of using them as temporary instruments,
we identify ourselves with them.

Please do not look to my life, but take me
even as a lamppost on the road
that indicates the way,
but cannot walk the way itself.

After I am gone
no single person will be able completely to represent me.
But a little bit of me will live in many of you.
If each puts the cause first and himself last,
the vacuum will to a large extent be filled.

I Am You, You Are Me

The purpose of life is undoubtedly to know oneself.
We cannot do so unless we learn to identify ourselves
with all that lives.
The instrument of this knowledge
is boundless, selfless service.

We must feel one with all.

And I have discovered
that we never give
without receiving
consciously
or unconsciously.

Wealth and Sharing

Man falls from the pursuit of the ideal
of plain living and high thinking
the moment he multiplies his daily wants.
History gives ample proof of this.
Man's happiness lies in contentment.
He who is discontented, however much he possesses,
becomes a slave to his own desires. . . .
To be free or to be a slave lies in his own hands.

If there were no greed,
there would be no occasion for armaments.
The principle of non-violence necessitates complete abstention
from exploitation in any form.
As soon as the spirit of exploitation is gone,
armaments will be felt as a positively unbearable burden.
Real disarmament cannot come
unless the nations of the world cease to exploit one another.
A violent and bloody revolution is a certainty one day,
unless there is a voluntary abdication of riches—
and the power that riches give—
and a distribution of the wealth for the common good.

Earth has enough for man's need
but not for man's greed.

If each retained possession
of only what he needed,
no one would be in want
and all would live in contentment.

The Price of Wealth

The economics
that disregard moral and sentimental considerations
are waxworks that, being lifelike,
still lack the life of the living flesh.
At every crucial moment
these newfangled economic laws
have broken down in practice.
And nations or individuals
who accept them as guiding maxims
must perish.

In industrial society . . .
man is made to obey the machine.
The wealthy and the middle classes become helpless
and parasitic of the working classes.
And the latter become so specialized
that they also become helpless.
The cities become parasitic on the country,
industrial nations upon agricultural nations,
governments upon the people they govern. . . .
People even become parasitic in regard to their recreation:
they want to be amused instead of amusing themselves.

The people are becoming poorer
economically, mentally, and morally.
They are fast losing the will to work,
to think, and even to live.

This mad rush for wealth must cease,
and the laborer must be assured
not only of a living wage
but of a daily task
that is not mere drudgery.

Machines and Life

The supreme consideration is man.
The machine should not tend to make atrophied
the limbs of man.

It is beneath human dignity to lose one's individuality
and become a mere cog in the machine.
I want every individual to become a full-blooded,
fully developed member of society.

If capital is power, so is work.
Either power can be used
destructively or creatively.

The body itself is but an extraordinary
delicately constructed machine....
We are destroying these matchless living machines,
our bodies,
and trying to substitute lifeless machinery for them,
machines that would displace human labor...
and concentrate power in a few hands.

What I object to
is the "craze"
for what they call
labor-saving machinery.
Men go on "saving labor"
till thousands are without work
and thrown on the open streets
to die of starvation.

I am not against machinery as such,
but I am totally opposed to it when it masters us.

Today machinery merely helps a few
to ride on the backs of millions.
The impetus behind it all
is not the philanthropy to save labor
but greed.

Hand and Civilization

Idleness, whether enforced or voluntary,
is killing the very soul of the nation. . . .
It is a tragedy of the first magnitude that millions
have ceased to use their hands as hands.
Nature is revenging herself upon us
with terrible effect
for this criminal waste of the gift she has bestowed
upon us human beings. . . .
It is the exquisite mechanism of the hands
that, among a few other things,
separates us from the beast.

Why am I turning back the course of modern civilization
when I ask the villager to grind his own meal
and eat it whole,
including the nourishing bran?. . .
Am I turning back the course of modern civilization
when I ask the villager not merely to grow raw produce,
but to turn it into marketable products?

Surely, modern civilization is not millennia old.
We can almost give its birth an exact date. . . .
There is a growing body of enlightened opinion
which distrusts Western civilization,
which has insatiable material ambition at one end
and consequent war at the other.

It is only the handicraft civilization that will endure
and stand the test of time.
But it can do so only
if we can correlate the intellect with the hand.

Work

All labor,
when done intelligently and for some high purpose
becomes at once re-creation and recreation.

In our country
manual labor is regarded as a low occupation....
We should spin, therefore,
if only to guard against the pernicious assumption
that toilers are lower on the social scale.

Every profession has been degraded to mean a career.
We become lawyers, doctors, and schoolmasters
not to serve our countrymen
but to bring ourselves money.

Work and culture cannot be separated.
Man cannot develop his mind
by simply writing and making speeches all day long.

I cannot imagine anything nobler
than that for, say, one hour in the day
we should do the labor the poor must do,
and thus identify ourselves with them
and, through them,
with all mankind.

Interdependence

If man . . . could so place himself as to be
absolutely above all dependence on his fellow beings
he would become so proud and arrogant
as to be a veritable burden and nuisance to the world.
Dependence on society
teaches the lessons of humanity.

A man cannot become self-sufficient . . .
whether from the growing of the cotton
to the spinning of the yarn. . . .
He has at some stage or other
to take the aid of the members of his family.
And if one may take help from one's own family,
why not from one's neighbors?
Or otherwise, what is the significance of the great saying
"The world is my family"?

The better mind of the world desires today
not absolutely independent states
warring one against the other,
but a federation of friendly interdependent states.

Isolated independence is not the goal of world states.
It is voluntary interdependence.

Interdependence is and ought to be
as much the ideal of man as self-sufficiency.
Man is a social being.
Without interrelation with society
he cannot realize his oneness with the universe
or suppress his egotism.

Serene Homes and Villages

Simple homes
from which there is nothing to take away
require no policing;
the palaces of the rich must have
strong guards to protect them....
So must huge factories.

Sooner or later
the fact must be recognized that people
will have to live in villages,
not in towns,
in huts,
not in palaces.
Millions of people will never be able to live
in peace with each other in towns and in palaces.

Village Democracy

My idea of village self-rule is a complete republic
independent of its neighbors for its own vital wants.
It should be built of material
obtainable within a radius of five miles of it.
Its first concern will be to grow its own grain, vegetable and fruit,
and its own homespun material.
It will have cottages with sufficient light and ventilation,
wells according to its needs and accessible to all,
a reserve for its cattle,
recreation and playground for adults and children.
The village will maintain a theater, school, and public hall.
There will be no castes.
Here there is a perfect democracy
based upon individual freedom.
It will have houses of worship for all,
also a common meeting place.
No one will be idle, no one will wallow in luxury.
Men and women will be free
and able to hold their own against anyone in the world.

My notion of democracy is that under it the weakest should
have the same opportunity as the strongest.

Real self-rule will come
not by the acquisition of authority by a few,
but by the capacity of all
to resist authority when abused.

True democracy cannot be worked by twenty men
sitting at the center.
It has to be worked from below
by the people of every village.

Parliaments have no power or even existence
independently of the people....
Every citizen therefore renders himself responsible
for every act of his government.

Liberty never meant the license to do anything at will.

Means and Ends

The means can be likened to a seed,
the end to a tree,
and there is just the same inviolable connection
between the means and the end
as there is between the seed and the tree.

They say: "Means are, after all, just means."
I would say: "Means are, after all, everything."
As the means, so the end.
Violent means will give violent independence....
There is no wall of separation between means and end.
If we take care of the means,
we are bound to reach the end sooner or later.

Means and ends
are convertible terms in my philosophy of life.

Man cannot do right in one department of life
whilst he is occupied in doing wrong
in another department.
Life is one indivisible whole.

Satyagraha
The Power of Non-Violence

Truth (satya) implies love,
and firmness (agraha)
serves as a synonym for force.
I thus began to call the Indian movement satyagraha;
that is to say, the force which is born of truth and love,
or non-violence.

It is my wife who taught me non-violence.
Her obstinate resistance, on one hand,
and her serene acceptance of the suffering
my stupidity inflicted on her
made me stop believing that nature had given me a right
to dominate her.
From that moment onward,
she became my teacher of satyagraha.

In my humble opinion, non-cooperation with evil
is as much a duty as is cooperation with good.
Non-violence implies voluntary submission
to the penalty for non-cooperation with evil.

Non-violence and cowardice go ill together....
Possession of arms implies an element of fear, if not cowardice.
But true non-violence is an impossibility
without the possession of utter fearlessness.

If all the mice in the world
resolved that they would no more fear the cat
but instead all ran into her mouth,
the mice would live.

Civil Disobedience

Civil disobedience ... becomes a sacred duty
when the state becomes lawless
or corrupt.
And a citizen who barters with such a state
shares its corruption or lawlessness.

Civil disobedience, mass or individual,
is a full substitute for armed revolt....
Mankind has to eliminate violence
only through non-violence.

Civil disobedience is the inherent right of a citizen.
He dare not give it up without ceasing to be a man.
Civil disobedience is never followed by anarchy,
criminal disobedience can lead to it.
Every state puts down criminal disobedience by force:
it perishes, if it does not.
But to put down civil disobedience
is to attempt to imprison conscience.

Passive resisters cannot—must not—
lose faith in themselves or in their mission
because they may be in a minority. . . .
All reform has been brought about by the action of minorities
in all countries and under all climes.

Disobedience, to be civil, requires discipline,
thought, care, attention.
It has to be open and non-violent.

Training is necessary as well for civil disobedience
as for armed revolt.
Only the ways are different.

Joy lies in the struggle,
in the attempt,
in the suffering involved,
not in the victory itself.

Who enjoys freedom afterward
when whole divisions of armed soldiers
rush into a hailstorm of bullets to be mown down?
But in the case of non-violence,
everybody seems to start with the assumption
that the non-violent method
must be set down as a failure
unless he himself at least
lives to enjoy the success thereof.

Love

The more efficient a force is, the more silent and subtle it is.
Love is the subtlest force in the world.

The law of love governs the world.
Life persists in the face of death.
The universe continues
in spite of destruction incessantly going on.
Truth triumphs over untruth.
Love conquers hate.

True love transfers itself
from the body to the dweller within,
and then necessarily realizes the oneness of all life
inhabiting numberless bodies.

Man does not live by destruction,
self-love compels regard for others.
Nations cohere only because there is mutual regard
among the individuals composing them.
Some day we must extend the national law to the universe
even as we have extended the family law
to form nations—a larger family.

Scientists tell us
that without the presence of the cohesive force
amongst the atoms that comprise this globe of ours
it would crumble to pieces and we would cease to exist.
And even as there is a cohesive force in blind matter
so must there be one in all things animate.
And the name
for that cohesive force among animate beings
is love.

Religion

All religions are more or less true,
All proceed from the same God, but all are imperfect
because they come down to us
through imperfect human instrumentality.

I believe in the absolute oneness of God
and therefore of humanity.
What if we have many bodies?
We have but one soul.
The rays of the sun are many through reflection.
But they have the same source. . . .
I am endeavoring to see God through service of humanity,
for I know God is neither in heaven nor down below
but in everyone. . . .
The sum total of all that lives is God.
We may not be God, but we are of God
even as a little drop of water is of the ocean.

Faith is a function of the heart.
It must be enforced by reason.
The two are not antagonistic, as some think.
The more intense one's faith is,
the more it whets one's reason.
When faith becomes blind, it dies.

What is faith worth
if it is not translated into action?

Religions are different roads
converging to the same point.
What does it matter that we take different roads
as long as we reach the same goal?
In reality there are as many religions
as there are individuals.
Mankind is one.

End or Beginning

Nature knows no mercy in dealing stern justice.
If we do not wake up before long,
we shall be wiped out of existence. . . .
Is it impossible to multiply the exceptions
so as to make them the rule? . . .
If we are to make progress, we must not repeat history
but make new history.

What is wanted
is deliberate giving up of violence out of strength.
To be able to do so requires imagination
coupled with a penetrating study of the world drift.
Today . . . we mistake for progress
the giddy dance which engages us from day to day.
We refuse to see that it is surely leading us to death.

If we cut off taking a necessary step
till everyone else is ready for it
we shall never move on.
We must have the courage to take the plunge
even if we are alone.
Many difficulties that deter us are imaginary.

We must refuse to wait for generations
to furnish us with a patient solution of a problem
which is ever-growing in seriousness.

If we make new discoveries and inventions
in the phenomenal world
must we declare our bankruptcy in the spiritual domain?
Must man always be brute first and man after,
if at all?

Remember Hope

Man often becomes what he believes himself to be.
If I keep saying to myself that I cannot do a certain thing
it is possible that I may end
by really becoming incapable of doing it.
On the contrary, if I have the belief that I can do it
I shall surely acquire the capacity to do it
even if I may not have had it at the beginning.

In this age of wonders no one will say
that a thing or an idea is worthless because it is new.
To say it is impossible because it is difficult
is again not in consonance with the spirit of the age.
Things undreamt of are daily being seen,
the impossible is ever becoming possible.
We are constantly being astonished, these days,
at the amazing discoveries in the field of violence.
I maintain that far more undreamt of
and seemingly impossible discoveries
will be made in the field of non-violence.

I have nothing new to teach the world.
Truth and non-violence are as old as the hills. . . .
I have not the shadow of a doubt that any man or woman
can achieve what I have if he or she would make the same effort
and cultivate the same hope and faith.

You must not lose faith in humanity.
If a few drops are dirty,
the ocean does not become dirty.

Gandhi and His Time

1869-1883
England, the cradle of the industrial revolution, is the world's most powerful nation. Following England's lead, the industrial nations—Western Europe, the United States, and Russia—accelerate their rate of colonization abroad.

On October 2, 1869, Mohandas K. Gandhi is born in Porbandar, a small principality on the northeast coast of India, "pearl of the British Empire." In 1883, at the age of thirteen, Gandhi marries twelve-year-old Kasturba. (Although their marriage lasted sixty-two years, Gandhi and Kasturba later fought against the tradition of child marriages.)

1888-1891
Feudalism ends in Japan as does much of the Native American resistance in the United States. Workers demonstrate for the eight-hour day.

Defying his caste and leaving behind his wife and baby son, on September 4, 1888, nineteen-year-old Gandhi sails to England, where he studies English law for three years, passes his examination, and enrolls in the High Court before sailing back to India in 1891.

1893-1914
The United States and Spain, Russia and Japan, and England and the Boers in South Africa each are at war. The Boxers rise against foreigners in China. The Congo and Morocco are ruthlessly colonized. Queen Victoria, the Empress of India, dies, and Marie Curie wins the Nobel prize for the discovery of radium.

The young lawyer Gandhi settles in South Africa to represent an Indian business firm in a lawsuit. Although intending to remain there for only the duration of the trial, Gandhi stays for twenty years. As a victim of racial discrimination, he organizes non-violent actions within his community, at which he proves to be an effective leader. Arrested, then freed, he starts a newspaper and two collective farms, one of which he names for Tolstoy, with whom he corresponds. In 1914, Gandhi, accompanied by Kasturba, leaves South Africa forever. He travels through India and to England, where he takes interest in the suffragettes and their demonstrations for the right to vote.

1914-1918
The First World War begins and ends. The Bolsheviks seize power through the Russian Revolution. Workers revolt in Europe. England gives women the right to vote.

Back in India, in 1915 Gandhi sets up an ashram (spiritual community) in Ahmedabad. He leads non-violent campaigns for the rights of indigo planters, peasants, and textile workers—for whom he initiates his first hunger strike. He edits two newspapers, an English-language weekly, *Young India*, and its Gujarati companion, *Navajivan*.

1920-1932
After the civil war and Lenin's death in Russia, Stalin ousts Trotsky and seizes power. Fascism and Nazism are on the rise. Colonial revolts are ruthlessly put down. The New York stock market crashes, and millions are unemployed during the Great Depression. Hitler becomes chancellor of Germany.

Gandhi is elected president of the All India Home Rule League and resolves to wear only a loincloth of homespun cotton to encourage the village spinners and weavers. He defies colonial rule through civil disobedience and non-cooperation campaigns and is imprisoned for two years for writing seditious articles in *Young India*. He organizes the Salt March in defiance to the British monopoly on salt. Sixty thousand people, including Gandhi, are arrested for collecting salt on the seashore. Released, he goes to London for the Second Round Table Conference about India, continues his non-violent campaigns, and is jailed again. During his prison term, he fasts to protest against separate electoral bills for the untouchables, whom he calls *Harijans*, children of God.

1933-1938
Franklin Roosevelt launches the New Deal in the United States. Stalin consolidates his grip on the Soviet Union, liquidates his opponents and the peasants who refuse collectivization, and forcefully industrializes the country. Hitler edicts racial laws, rearms Germany, creates concentration camps, and annexes Austria and Czechoslovakia. Japan attacks China, and Italy invades Ethiopia. Spain is divided by Civil War.

Gandhi starts a society and a newspaper called *Harijan* to end untouchability (and to replace *Young India*, which was closed by the government). He launches the All India Village Industries Association and escapes several attempts on his life. Kasturba is repeatedly imprisoned.

1939-1945
World War II begins and ends: 55,000,000 are killed, mostly civilians. The full horror of Hitler's extermination camps is revealed, and the United States drops the first and second atom bombs. The United Nations is created.

The non-violent disobedience campaigns reach their climax with the "Quit India" movement. Gandhi, Kasturba, and the leaders of the Congress Party are imprisoned by the British. Kasturba dies in jail. Gandhi pleads for the unity of India with Mohamed Ali Jinnah of the Muslim League. Violence erupts between Muslims and Hindus.

1946-1948
Greece and China are engaged in civil wars while liberation wars plague Africa and Asia. The Marshall Plan is adopted for ruined post-war Europe. The Cold War begins, as does the age of consumerism.

In spite of Gandhi's opposition to the partition of India, his fasts and marches to avoid bloodshed between Hindus and Muslims, the independence of India is proclaimed concurrently with the creation of Pakistan. Riots and massacres follow. On January 28, 1948, during a prayer meeting, Gandhi is murdered by a Hindu opposed to his conciliatory attitudes towards Muslims.

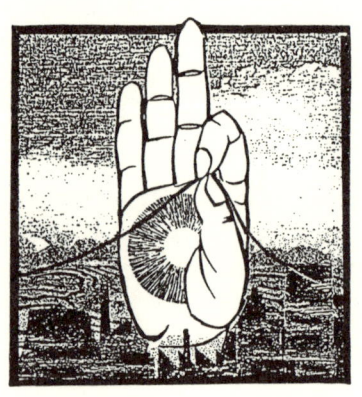

May love of your neighbor

be like cotton,

your garment in life

and in death

your shroud.

Song for Gandhi
Muslim musicians
Delhi 1947